MOMENTS
NOTICE

NICO
VASSILAKIS

Luna Bisonte Prods
2013

NICO VASSILAKIS

M O M E N T S   N O T I C E

A few of these images were previously published
in the following publications or blogs:

Next Poems
Rusty Toque
National Poetry Month
iARTista

The cover design is a collaboration by
C. Mehrl Bennett and Nico Vassilakis,
based on the first image in this book.

ISBN 978-1-938521-06-5

LUNA BISONTE PRODS
137 Leland Ave
Columbus, OH 43214-7505 U.S.A.

https://www.lulu.com/spotlight/lunabisonteprods

this is a visual poem

MOMENTS NOTICE G
uest tongue Invites lett
ers to cavort before vo
calization Just as the d
rawings they are A ba
ckdrop of black rubber
bands Between three
quasars and Take me t
o your robot leader Fl
ush Space Rivet x inte
rtwined with oh and by
and peg and be The g
ame ends as you're fac
ed with Writing your di
sease The sound of R
ococo Suck "Things
which coincide with on
e another equal one an

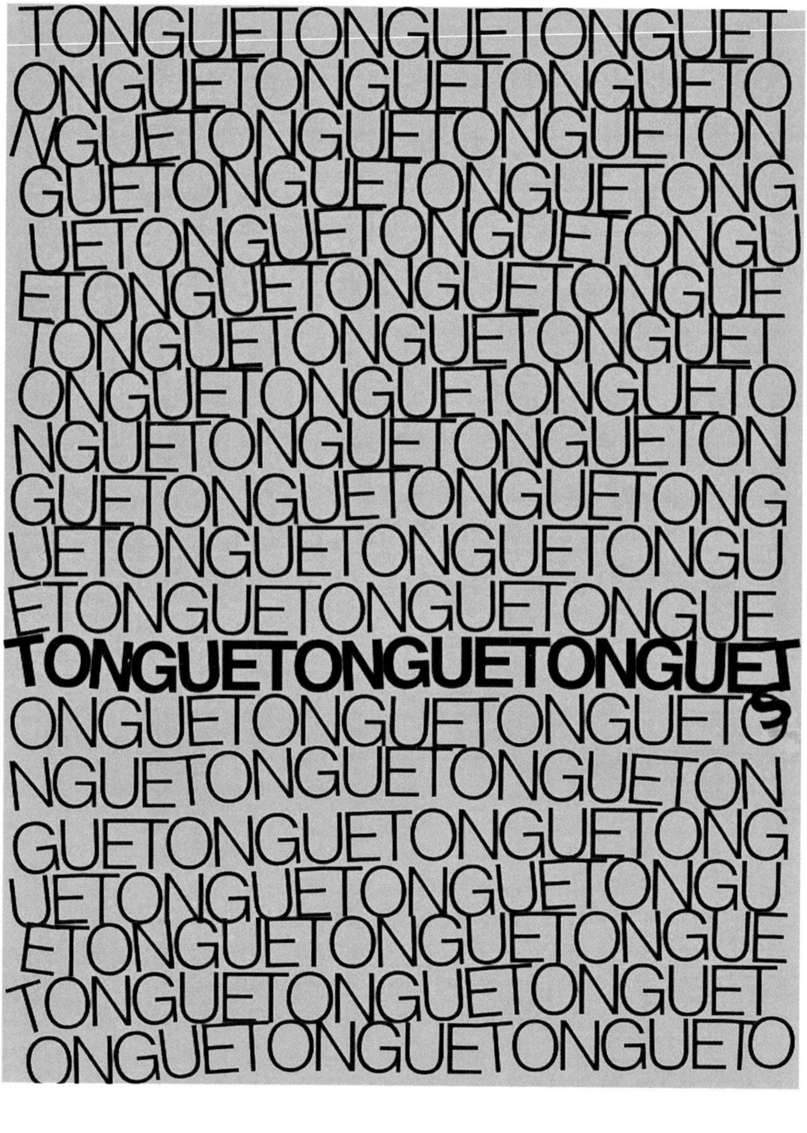
TONGUETONGUETONGUET
ONGUETONGUETONGUETO
NGUETONGUETONGUETON
GUETONGUETONGUETONG
UETONGUETONGUETONGU
ETONGUETONGUETONGUE
TONGUETONGUETONGUET
ONGUETONGUETONGUETO
NGUETONGUETONGUETON
GUETONGUETONGUETONG
UETONGUETONGUETONGU
ETONGUETONGUETONGUE
TONGUETONGUETONGUET
ONGUETONGUETONGUETO
NGUETONGUETONGUETON
GUETONGUETONGUETONG
UETONGUETONGUETONGU
ETONGUETONGUETONGUE
TONGUETONGUETONGUET
ONGUETONGUETONGUETO

9

between

three

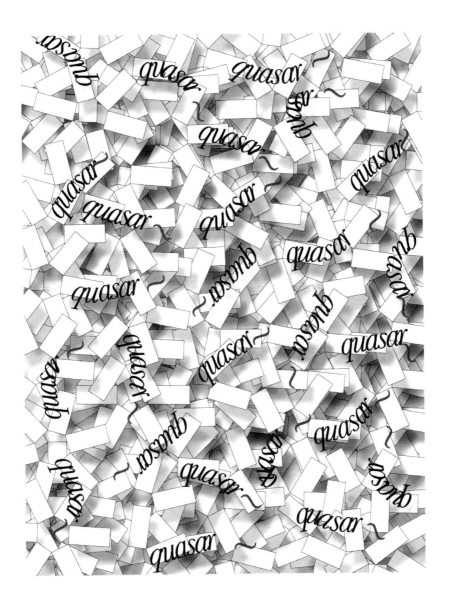

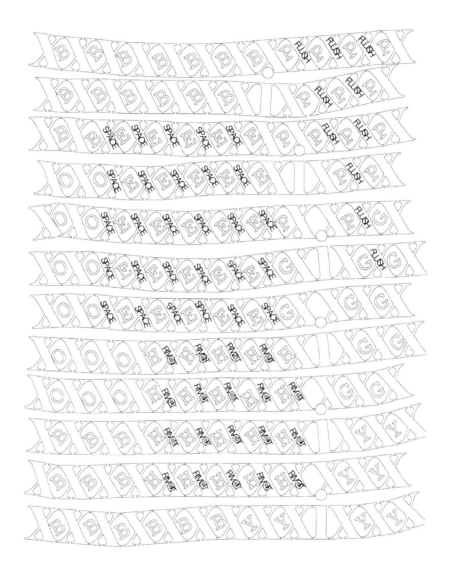

game end write your disease

Things which coincide with
one another equal one another.

other" The sound of U
RN URN Couched by 2
 yellow dots He's on hi
s way up But it's wron
g Ambition's wrong L
etters are sci-fi The wi
nd the numbers rain U
pon waking, I left the b
uilding Awaiting life or
a similar suspension
Letter salad Letter scie
nce Letters from space
 A trunk of lowercase
e's A cul de sac of scri
pt A hyphenated bridg
e of t's Moments notic

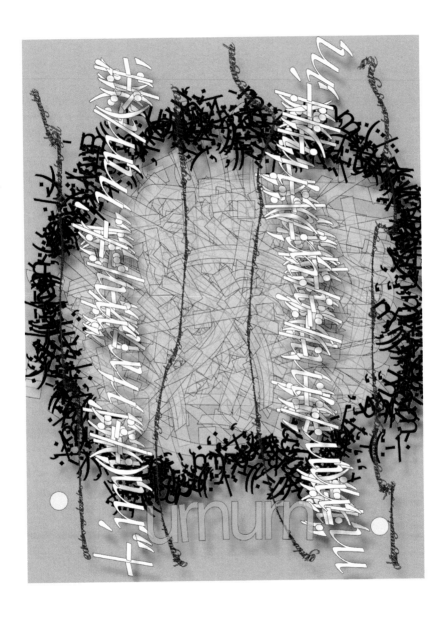

17

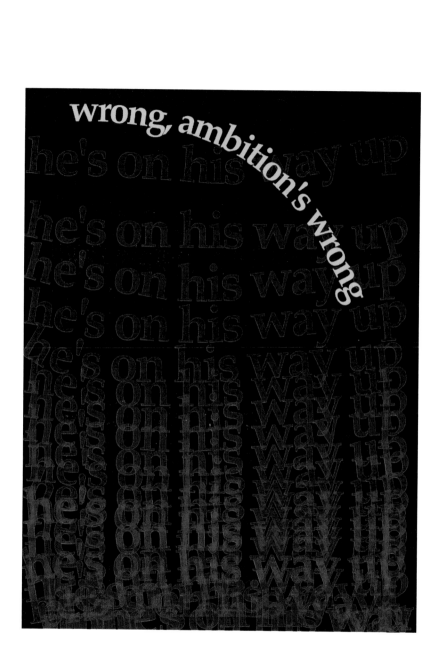

wrong ambition's wrong

he's on his way up
he's on his way up
he's on his way up
he's on his way up
he's on his way up
he's on his way up
he's on his way up
he's on his way up
he's on his way up
he's on his way up
he's on his way

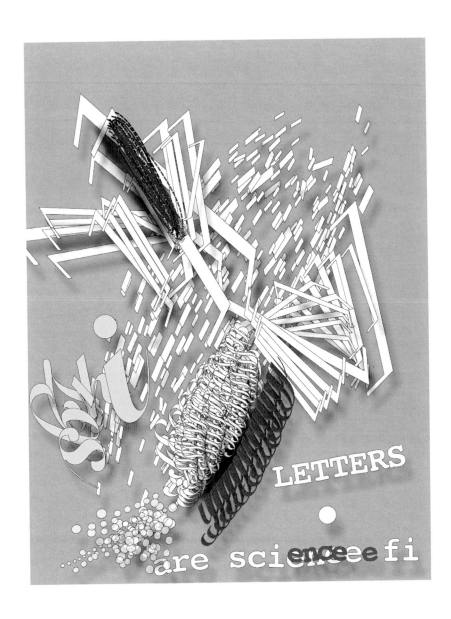

the wind the numbers rain

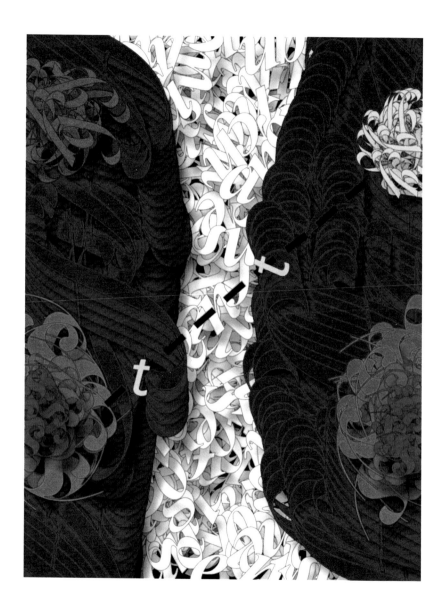

e The result of a short
exchange About weat
her Several indeciphe
rable or blocked phras
es I've stayed apace B
ut find I'm now ready T
o detach Trouble sho
oting the possessive A
postrophe This comin
g air This trouble fault
This erased This spent
 It's a language decisi
on With extra umlauts
Confronting language
By both acquiring and
Suppressing knowled

the result of a short exchange about weather

I've stayed apace but find
I'm now ready to detac *h*

possessive

troublesse

30

ge After language Is th
is error Afterthought You
ou notice pause In a jo
yful amoebic glance A
n H in darkness Sinkin
g through a crack in ic
e 2 rescues on the way
Each rescue an optica
l illusion A magnified
microbe With three me
chanical legs Encased
in pencil skin A target i
s acquired As material
congeals Absorbed th
rough the air The air th
rough the air The cent

34

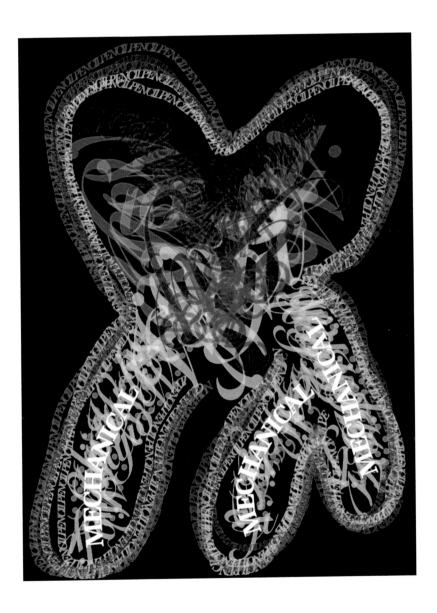

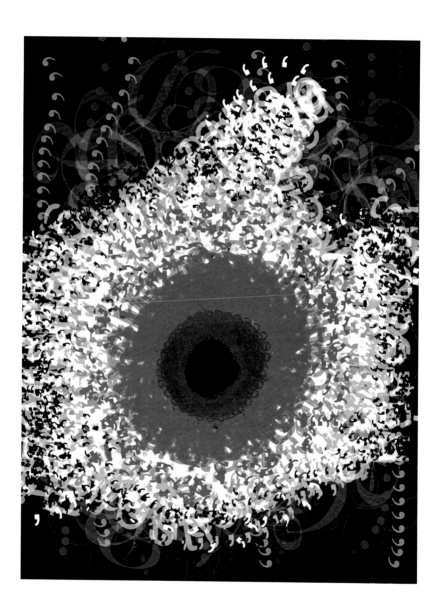

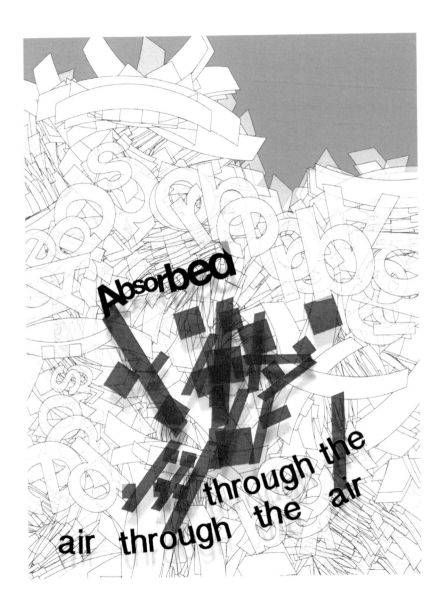

Absorbed through the air through the air

al nerve of language Is
free space Paragraph
language inside the se
ntence Is a Gertrude h
at Moments notice A s
talk of decorative Lette
r fruit The crime scene
 Deviates at the rupture
A composition Left ot
herwise In the noise W
e are hearing letters In
the house We hear lett
ers Contrive a bounda
ry And halve it A neura
l blockage An outside f
orest Spotted with un
wanted Filigree And t

inside the sentence

Gertrude Ha~

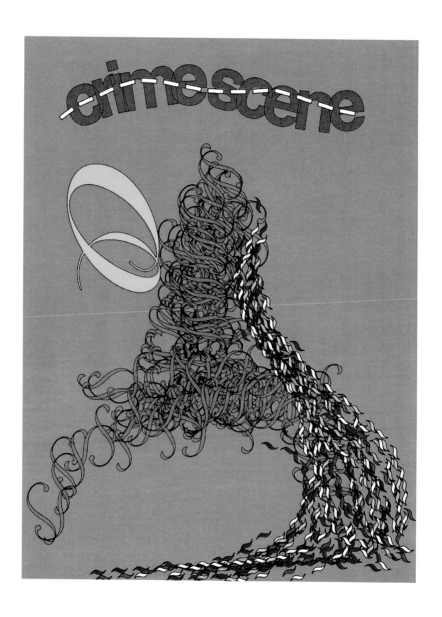

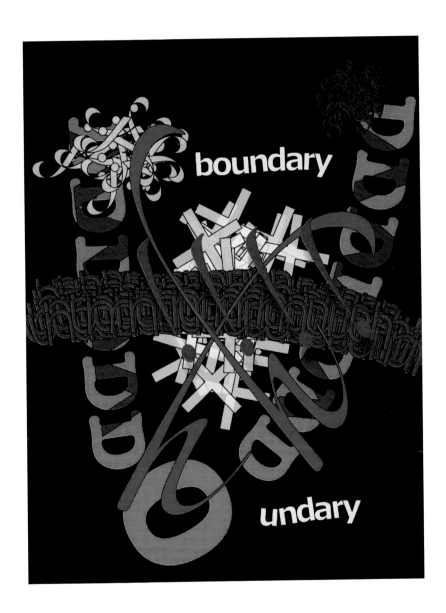

boundary

undary

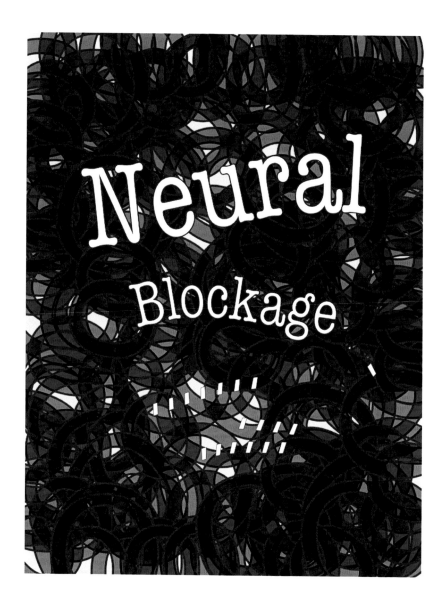

49

hat Will you be denied
? Yes, you will be deni
ed - but that's okay Ca
ution the f, the myriad l
owercase t Thwart is d
irection A decision one
 makes 99 or double b
b An ampersand will st
retch Beyond its surfa
ce The semi colon as
example A bi-axial cod
ex To be To be larger
To be off to the side To
 be declaration Three
compositional circles
Over white sticks mo

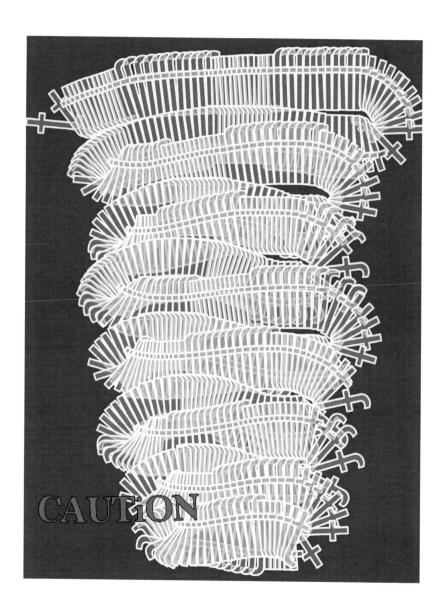

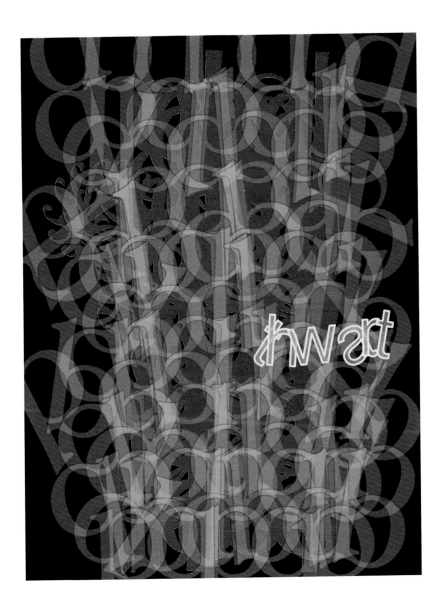

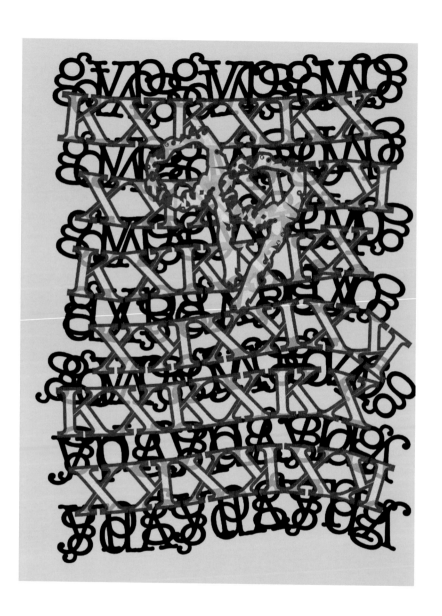

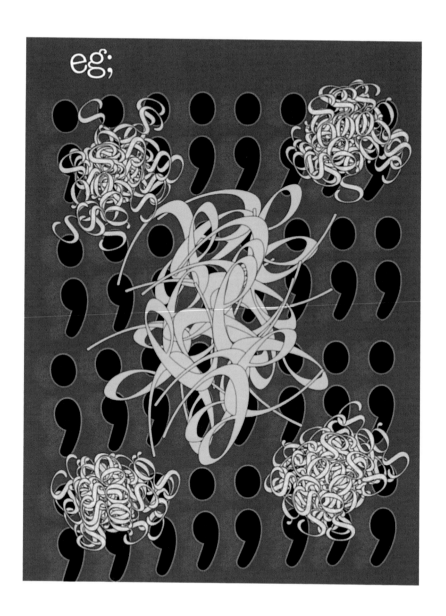

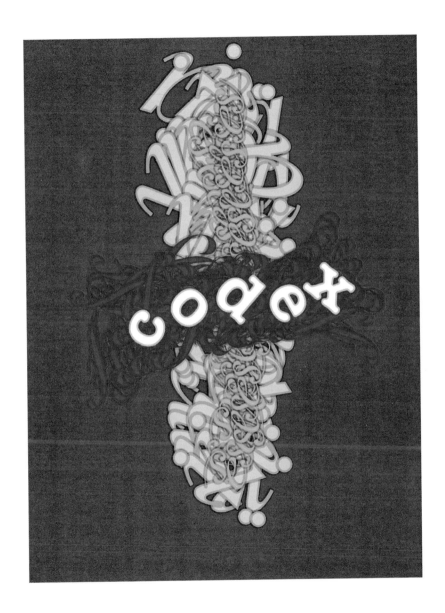

ments notice We are
way behind weather M
ultiple layers of weathe
r And the tenfold paren
thesis Dear Pencil Hell
o Hyphenation Though
erasure feeds on histo
ry Sincerely, Keyboard
Leave this place Silen
ce is coming The pres
ent tense and Silence i
s coming You will leav
e this place Air swirl T
he central nerve is free
space Positive and ne
gative concrete Friend

PARE
NTHE
TICAE

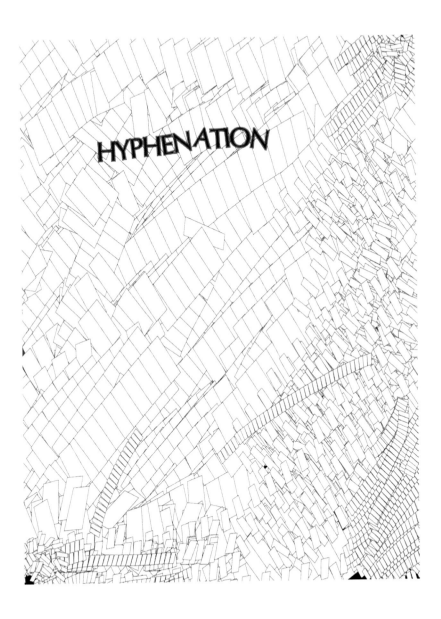

HYPHENATION

66

silence is coming

LEAVE THIS PLACE LEAVE THIS PLACE LEAVE THIS PLACE LEAVE THIS PLACE LEAVE THIS PLACE LEAVE THIS PLACE LEAVE THIS PLACE

silence is coming

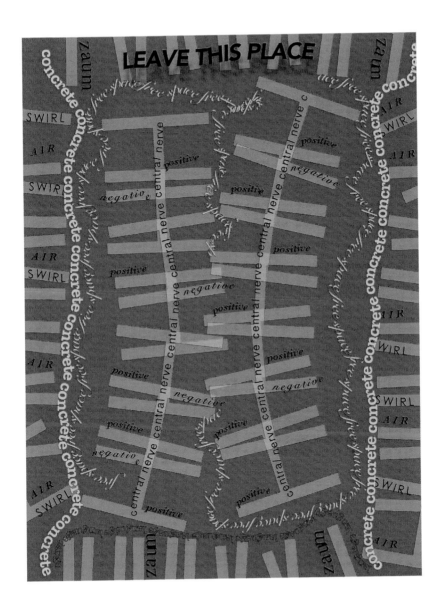

let yourself slip throug
h Stop being boring St
op boring More Sucker
 punch sushi sonnet It
is essentially a house t
ext An oversized YES

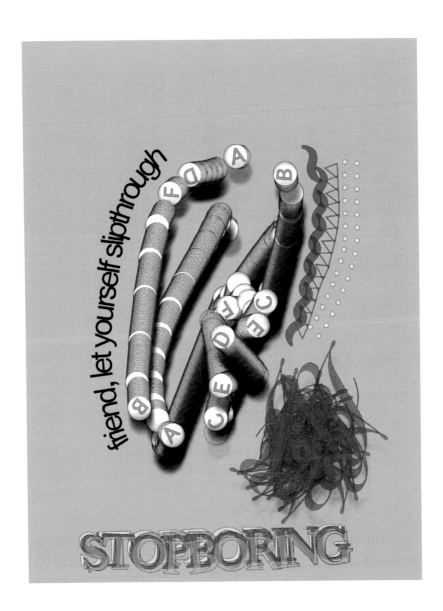

sucker
punch
sushi
sonnet

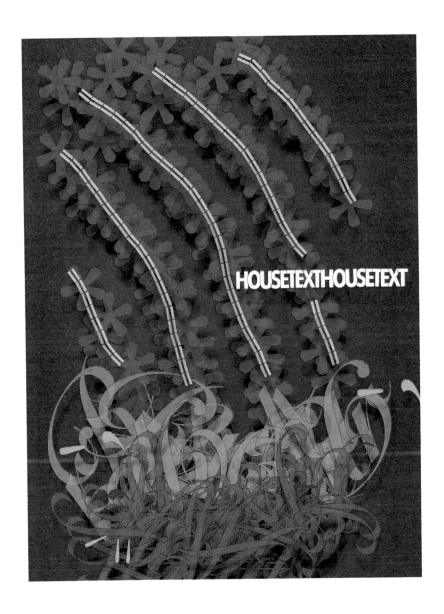

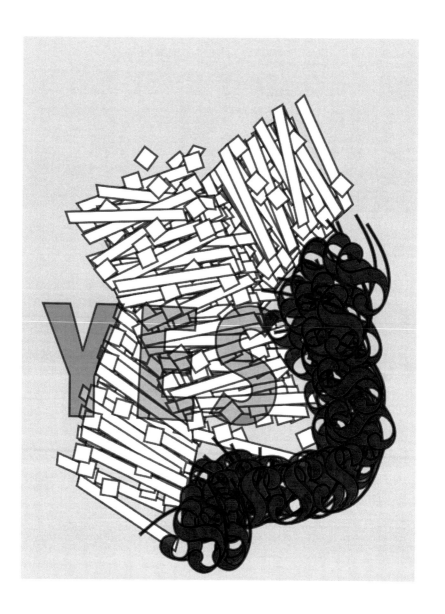